TO:

....

FROM:

....

DATE:

....

Compiled by Kathy Shutt.

ISBN 978-1-61626-193-1

Cover and interior design: ThinkPen Design

Published by Barbour Publishing, Inc., P.O. Box 719, Uhrichsville, Ohio 44683, www.barbourbooks.com

Our mission is to publish and distribute inspirational products offering exceptional value and biblical encouragement to the masses.

Member of the
Evangelical Christian
Publishers Association

Printed in Malaysia.

In
Celebration
of You
Mom

BARBOUR
PUBLISHING

Mom—a simple little word that conjures up
fond memories, warm feelings,
and a sense of wonder at all she
manages to accomplish.

REBECCA GERMANY

When it comes to love, *Mom's* the word.

UNKNOWN

A mother's love perceives no impossibilities.

CORNELIA PADDOCK

People are what their mothers make them.

RALPH WALDO EMERSON

To give without any reward,
or any notice, has a special quality of its own.

ANNE MORROW LINDBERGH

Mother love is the fuel that enables a normal human being to do the impossible.

UNKNOWN

Through the ages no nation has had a better friend than the mother who taught her child to pray.

UNKNOWN

The mother's heart is the child's schoolroom.

HENRY WARD BEECHER

*A mother is not a person to lean on,
but a person to make leaning unnecessary.*

DOROTHY CANFIELD FISHER

It is not our exalted feelings, it is our
sentiments that build the necessary home.

ELIZABETH BOWEN

*There is no influence so powerful
as that of a mother.*

SARAH JOSEPHA HALE

The joy of the LORD is your strength.

NEHEMIAH 8:10 KJV

A mother laughs our laughs,
sheds our tears, returns our love,
fears our fears. She lives our joys,
cares our cares, and all our hopes
and dreams she shares.

UNKNOWN

A mother's love and prayers and tears are
seldom lost on even the most wayward child.

A. E. DAVIS

*When you lead your sons and daughters
in the good way, let your words be
tender and caressing, in terms of
discipline that wins the heart's assent.*

ELIJAH BEN SOLOMON ZALMAN

A mother's love for her child is like
nothing else in the world. It knows no law,
no pity; it dares all things and crushes down
remorselessly all that stands in its path.

AGATHA CHRISTIE

Mother is the bank where we deposit
all our hurts and worries.

UNKNOWN

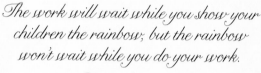

The work will wait while you show your children the rainbow; but the rainbow won't wait while you do your work.

PATRICIA CLAFFORD

The greatest teacher is not experience;
it is example.

JOHN CROYLE

"I will pour out my Spirit on your offspring, and my blessing on your descendants."

Isaiah 44:3 NIV

You will find, as you look back upon your life, that the moments when you have really lived are the moments when you have done things in the spirit of love.

HENRY DRUMMOND

To love abundantly is to live abundantly, and to love forever is to live forever.

ANONYMOUS

Through all of motherhood's joys and
sorrows, fulfillment and frustration,
we have a companion who never leaves us,
whether we sense His presence or not.
He smiles and laughs with us; He cries with
us and understands our frustrations.
In every aspect of a mother's
heart, we find images of this holy
companion. He never leaves us.

ELLYN SANNA

The heart of a mother is a deep
abyss at the bottom of which you
will always find forgiveness.

HONORÈ DE BALZAC

I remember my mother's prayers,
and they have always followed me.
They have clung to me all my life.

ABRAHAM LINCOLN

My mother was the source from which
I derived the guiding principles of my life.

JOHN WESLEY

Nothing you do for children is ever wasted.
They seem not to notice us,
hovering, averting our eyes,
and they seldom offer thanks,
but what we do for them is never wasted.

GARRISON KEILLOR

*Some mothers are kissing mothers
and some are scolding mothers,
but it is love just the same, and most
mothers kiss and scold together.*

PEARL S. BUCK

*Faith is being sure of what we hope for
and certain of what we do not see.*

Hebrews 11:1 niv

*Mother is the name of God in the
lips and mouths of little children.*

WILLIAM MAKEPEACE THACKERAY

Happy the home when God is there,
And love fills every breast;
When one their wish, and one their prayer,
And one their heavenly rest.
Happy is the home where Jesus' Name
Is sweet to every ear;
Where children early speak His fame,
And parents hold Him dear.

HENRY WARE JR.

Worry never robs tomorrow
of its sorrow; it only saps
today of its strength.
A. J. CRONIN

Do not lose courage in considering
your imperfections,
but instantly set about remedying
them—every day begin the task anew.

FRANCIS DE SALES

*Do what you can,
with what you have, where you are.*

THEODORE ROOSEVELT

Rejecting things because they are
old-fashioned would rule out the sun
and the moon, and a mother's love.

UNKNOWN

*And through the years, a mother has
been all that's sweet and good,
For there's a bit of God and love
in all true motherhood.*

HELEN STEINER RICE

Where can one better be than the
bosom of one's own family?

FRENCH PROVERB

*Be an example to all believers in what
you say, in the way you live,
in your love, your faith, and your purity.*

1 Timothy 4:12 nlt

Train your child in the way in which you
know you should have gone yourself.

CHARLES H. SPURGEON

*Let us be grateful to the people who
make us happy—they are the charming
gardeners who make our souls blossom.*

MARCEL PROUST

Love children especially. . . .
They live to soften and purify our hearts.

FYODOR DOSTOYEVSKY

Where there is room in the heart,
there is always room in the house.

THOMAS MORE

Where the soul is full of peace and joy,
outward surroundings and circumstances
are of comparatively little account.

HANNAH WHITALL SMITH

Happiness is the atmosphere in
which all good affections grow.

ANNA ELIZA BRAY

When we start to count flowers,
We cease to count weeds;
When we start to count blessings,
We cease to count needs;
When we start to count laughter,
We cease to count tears;
When we start to count memories,
We cease to count years.

Unknown

God provides resting places as well
as working places. Rest, then,
and be thankful when He brings
you wearied to a wayside well.

L. B. COWMAN

*Whoever walks toward God one step,
God runs toward him two.*

JEWISH PROVERB

We were not sent into this world
to do anything into which we
cannot put our hearts.

JOHN RUSKIN

The most important piece of clothing you must wear is love. Love is what binds us all together in perfect harmony.

Colossians 3:14 nlt

A family holds hands and sticks together.

UNKNOWN

A small house will hold as much
happiness as a big one.

UNKNOWN

In order to manage children well,
we must borrow their eyes and their
hearts, and feel as they do,
and judge them from their own point of view.

EUGÉNIE DE GUÉRIN

*It is love that asks, that seeks,
that knocks, that finds, and that
is faithful to what it finds.*

AUGUSTINE

A family is a little world created by love.

UNKNOWN

A mother's love lives on. . . .
She remembers. . .her child's merry
laugh, the joyful shout of his childhood,
the opening promise of his youth.

Washington Irving

*Allow children to be happy in
their own way, for what better
way will they ever find?*

Samuel Johnson

Home is the one place in all this world
where hearts are sure of each other.

FREDERICK W. ROBERTSON

To a child, love is spelled T-I-M-E.

UNKNOWN

A mother's love endures through all.

WASHINGTON IRVING

But the fruit of the Spirit is love, joy, peace, patience, kindness, goodness, faithfulness, gentleness and self-control.

Galatians 5:22 niv

*Give a little love to a child and
you get a great deal back.*

JOHN RUSKIN

Sometimes I wonder—*what kind of example
am I leaving my children? What will they write
on my tombstone or say about me after I'm
gone?* . . . Hopefully my epitaph will read
something like this: "She hated folding
laundry but liked to fold us in her arms."

DENA DYER

No one is useless in this world who lightens the burdens of it for another.

CHARLES DICKENS

A mother understands what
a child does not say.

JEWISH PROVERB

Holy as heaven a mother's tender love,
the love of many prayers and many tears
which changes not with dim, declining years.

CAROLINE NORTON

A mother is she who can take the place of all others but whose place no one else can take.

CARDINAL MERMILLOD

Children are the sum of what mothers contribute to their lives.

UNKNOWN

Charm is deceptive, and beauty is fleeting;
but a woman who fears the
Lord is to be praised.

PROVERBS 31:30 NIV

*God pardons like a mother who kisses
the offense into everlasting forgiveness.*

HENRY WARD BEECHER

Other things may change us,
but we start and end with the family.

ANTHONY BRANDT

The mother is everything—she is our consolation in sorrow, our hope in misery, and strength in weakness. She is the source of love, mercy, sympathy, and forgiveness.

KHALIL GIBRAN

The family is the only institution in the world where the kingdom of God can actually begin.

PLATO

The Christian home is the Master's workshop where the process of character-molding is silently, lovingly, faithfully, and successfully carried on.

RICHARD MONCKTON MILNES

Your greatest pleasure is that which rebounds from hearts that you have made glad.

HENRY WARD BEECHER

To laugh often and love much;
to win the respect of intelligent people and
the affection of children. . .to appreciate
beauty; to find the best in others. . .to know
even one life has breathed easier because
you have lived. That is to have succeeded.

RALPH WALDO EMERSON

*True serenity comes when we
give ourselves to God.*

ELLYN SANNA

Children are a gift from the LORD;
they are a reward from him.

Psalm 127:3 nlt

The mother love is like God's love;
He loves us not because we are lovable,
but because it is His nature to love,
and because we are His children.

EARL RINEY

*To be a mother is a woman's greatest
vocation in life. She is a partner with God.*

SPENCER W. KIMBALL

Her dignity consists in being unknown
to the world; her glory is in the
esteem of her husband; her pleasures
in the happiness of her family.

Jean-Jacques Rousseau

*A child needs a mother more than
all the things money can buy.*

Ezra Taft Benson

The imprint of the mother remains
forever on the life of the child.

Unknown

The power of a mother's prayers
could stand an army on its ear.

ELIZABETH DEHAVEN

Maternal love: a miraculous substance
which God multiplies as He divides it.

VICTOR HUGO

The mother loves her child most divinely,
not when she surrounds him with comfort
and anticipates his wants, but when she
resolutely holds him to the highest standards
and is content with nothing less than his best.

HAMILTON WRIGHT MABIE

*Mothers have as powerful an influence
over the welfare of future generations
as all other causes combined.*

JOHN ABBOT

A kindhearted woman gains respect.

PROVERBS 11:16 NIV

I have held many things in my hands and I have lost them all; but whatever I have placed in God's hands, that I still possess.

MARTIN LUTHER

There was never a great man who had not a great mother.

OLIVE SCHREINER

Love begins by taking care of the closest ones—the ones at home.

MOTHER TERESA

Many make the household,
but only one the home.

JAMES RUSSELL LOWELL

The hardest job you will ever
love is being a mother.

UNKNOWN

A mother's love is like a circle.
It has no beginning and no ending.
It keeps going around and around,
ever expanding, touching everyone
who comes in contact with it.

UNKNOWN

A happy child has a joyful mother.

WANDA E. BRUNSTETTER

A mother. . .will cling to us, and endeavor
by her kind precepts and counsels to
dissipate the clouds of darkness,
and cause peace to return to our hearts.

WASHINGTON IRVING

Love each other as if your life depended on it.
Love makes up for practically anything.

1 PETER 4:8 MSG

When God thought of mother,
He must have laughed with satisfaction,
and framed it quickly—so rich,
so deep, so divine, so full of soul, power,
and beauty was the conception!

HENRY WARD BEECHER

There is a religion in all deep love,
but the love of a mother is the veil
of a softer light between the heart
and the heavenly Father.

SAMUEL TAYLOR COLERIDGE

If you would have your children to
walk honorably through the world,
you must not attempt to clear the stones
from their path, but teach them to
walk firmly over them—not insist
upon leading them by the hand,
but let them learn to go alone.

ANNE BRONTË

The riches that are in the
heart cannot be stolen.

RUSSIAN PROVERB

Children make love stronger,
days shorter, nights longer, bankrolls smaller,
homes happier, clothes shabbier,
the past forgotten, and the
future worth living for.

UNKNOWN

*No joy is so sublimely affecting as the joy of
a mother at the good fortune of her child.*

JEAN PAUL RICHTER

It's the little things that make up the
richest part of the tapestry of our lives.

UNKNOWN

God sends us children. . .to enlarge our
hearts, to make us unselfish and full
of kindly sympathies and affections,
to give our souls higher aims, to
call out all our faculties to extended
enterprise and exertion; to bring round
our fireside bright faces and happy
smiles, and loving, tender hearts.

MARY HOWITT

A rich child often sits in a poor mother's lap.

DANISH PROVERB

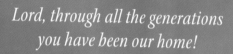

Lord, through all the generations
you have been our home!

PSALM 90:1 NLT

There is an enduring tenderness in the love of a mother to a child that transcends all other affections of the heart.

WASHINGTON IRVING

The present time is the most precious.

THOMAS À KEMPIS

A mother's love is the heart of the home.
Her children's sense of security
and self-worth is found there.

UNKNOWN

Mother's love grows by giving.
CHARLES LAMB

There are only two lasting bequests
we can hope to give our children.
One is roots; and the other, wings.

HODDING CARTER

When you get into a tight place and everything goes against you, till it seems as though you could not hang on a minute longer, never give up then, for that is just the place and time that the tide will turn.

HARRIET BEECHER STOWE

No ordinary work done by a man is either as hard or as responsible as the work of a woman who is bringing up a family of small children.

THEODORE ROOSEVELT

There is nothing but God's grace. We walk upon it; we breathe it; we live and die by it; it makes the nails and axles of the universe.

ROBERT LOUIS STEVENSON

A mother is the one through whom God whispers love to His little children.

UNKNOWN

Mother—in this consists the glory and the most precious ornament of woman.

MARTIN LUTHER

I thank God for you every day, Mom!
Just having you in my life
is reason to celebrate!